# RESET

*Cynnamon Clinton*

Copyright © 2025 by Cynnamon Clinton

All rights reserved. This book or any portion thereof may not be reproduced or used in any manner whatsoever without the express written permission of the publisher except for the use of brief quotations in a book review.

Printed in the United States of America

First Edition, 2025

PAPERBACK ISBN: 979-8-3482-8948-5

EBOOK ISBN: 979-8-3482-8949-2

Red Pen Edits and Consulting

www.redpeneditsllc.com

# DEDICATIONS

**RESET** is dedicated to individuals who have experienced childhood and relational trauma. It is dedicated to those who have experienced the foster care system, any form of abuse or neglect, and those who find themselves in unhealthy cycles and may not know how to make the decisions necessary to come out of them. If you have ever questioned your identity, been labeled an at-risk youth, or find yourself needing to mature and develop socially, emotionally, and in overall character, this book is dedicated to you.

# TABLE OF CONTENTS

INTRODUCTION ......................................... 1

**CHAPTER 1**

REWIND .................................................... 3

**CHAPTER 2**

EVALUATE/REEAVALUATE ...................... 16

**CHAPTER 3**

RELEASE ................................................. 24

**CHAPTER 4**

RECOVER ............................................... 35

**CHAPTER 5**

RESET ..................................................... 40

**ABOUT THE AUTHOR** .............................. 44

# INTRODUCTION

It's Never Too Late To Start Over.

It's Never Too Late To Make Better Decisions.

It's Never Too Late To Rewrite Your Story.

**THE 6 R'S TO RESET YOUR THINKING, EMOTIONS AND ACTIONS**

In life, we have all gone through things we wish we did not have to go through. We have all made decisions we are not happy about or that have brought about unfavorable consequences. In this book, we will discuss The **6 R's** to **RESET** your thinking, emotions, and actions to help develop better methods in making everyday decisions, whether you are currently going through something unfavorable or would like to hone in on your everyday life skills.

First, let me start by saying you are not alone. Many times, it may seem as if you are the only one going through this thing we call life. TV, social media, and the entertainment world make us believe others surrounding us have it perfect while somehow, we manage to fall short. In reality, this is far from the truth.

Because we are constantly surrounded by these "perfect" images, it becomes easy to forget that prosperity or thriving in certain areas in life (relationships, career, academics, etc...) comes from one's knowledge, support, character, perspective, skills, and ability to persevere. Why are traits the real reason one can thrive and prosper in life? Well, each helps a person to make better decisions for themselves and others.

# CHAPTER 1
# REWIND

**Going Backwards To Move Forward**

**This chapter is entitled "REWIND" because it is intended to cause you, the reader, to write and revisit your story as far back as you can remember. This will allow you to see where you may have developed certain mindsets, behaviors, and beliefs, whether good or bad. Before you do that, I'd like to introduce you to my friend, Cameron.**

Cameron, an ambitious elementary school kid, full of life, had a smile that lit up every room he walked into and told laugh-inducing jokes to go with it. He made all A's on his report cards and loved competing against his classmates in school. He lived with his mother, a strong-willed and intelligent woman, and his older sister, a responsible and well-loved young lady that Cameron looked up to very much.

Cameron's father and mother were divorced, and his father had been out of the home for years living thousands of miles away. He remembers his father calling during the summer promising to pick him and his sister up to spend quality time with them, but their father never showed up. Cameron remembered feeling so rejected and worthless as a kid because his father did not seem to love him. Relatives would say, "Your father use to pick you up when you were playing in the front yard and take you to the Shop." The Shop is where the men in the community hung out and played pool. Sadly, Cameron had no memories of this. Cameron fantasized and hung onto the story throughout middle school hoping that one day his father, his knight in shining armour, would come rescue and protect him. His father never did. The truth was, every time his father called and made promises, it disappointed him more. With each call, each false promise his heart broke over and over. Relatives began to tell more stories.

Stories that revealed to the young boy his father's struggle with an addiction to alcohol.

One day, Cameron asked to call his father. His mother stopped watching her old western show and looked Cameron square in the eyes. "He knows you're alive. If he wants to talk to you, he will call." Cameron went to bed and cried all night thinking his mother was being so mean. Little did he know, his mother was trying to protect him from a cycle of disappointment. His mother, who had a very blunt way of communicating because she had learned to survive with him and his sister, did not understand the importance of taking time to explain everything to Cameron so he could learn to accept the situation better. He felt angry, he felt powerless, and he felt as if all the adults in his life were disappointing him.

In the midst of these immense feelings of disappointment, one of the males in Cameron's life, a family friend Cameron looked up to tremendously, began to sexually abuse him. Cameron was too ashamed to tell anyone because he knew he did not want to get the family friend in trouble, even as a kid. There was also a strong belief taught in his family to respect and never speak up towards or against adults. Cameron began to hold this painful secret, unaware it would later contribute to cycles of unhealthy decisions.

In his home, he saw his mother work two jobs while attending college to provide for him and his sister. He remembers his mother struggling financially, fighting against attorneys to save their home, and seeing the distressed look on his mother's face every time something would break and needed to be fixed. He remembers seeing men come around to seemingly date his mother, but never staying around despite how good his mother was to them. He remembers how he felt unsafe and how he began to hate his body and existence.

By the time he transitioned to middle school, he began acting out at school and turned to "the streets." When frustrated, he would blow up on the teacher by yelling and walking out of class. He began to have suicidal thoughts, hated himself, and would ask God why he was alive. The sweet and innocent boy who was once ambitious, full of life, and had the brightest smile one could ever see was no longer apparent. Well, on the outside at least. The truth is, he was still there. He just needed someone to show him love so he did not have to portray the hard character he only created to protect himself. "The streets" seemed to love, respect, and never disappoint Cameron, qualities he had never experienced before. Because of this, those associated with "the streets" started to become his family.

Cameron became promiscuous, and his grades went from all A's and B's to all F's and D's. He failed the 9th grade, and was soon placed in an alternative school as a result of his behavior. When he arrived at the alternative school, he realized he had lots in common with the kids there. Was it the bad attitudes or need to disrespect their environment? No, they were all hurt, disappointed by the adults in their lives and did not have the proper tools and support to navigate out of the war that had now begun inside of them.

Cameron's light seemed to dim more and more. He became very timid, but when angered, he blew up like the Incredible Hulk and never expressed himself healthily. He allowed others to take his power by following what they were doing and not having his own mind. It seemed as if what happened to him in his elementary years had now created a cycle that he did not know how to break out of. He began to sleep long hours, fight, disrespect others, continuously hang out with other troubled individuals because they gave him attention, and treated going from one sleeping partner to the next as his normal. He started wearing baggy clothes and pants that fell off his buttocks in attempts to look tough, receive respect, and cover up the years of pain and shame he endured throughout his life.

Throughout all of this, Cameron's mother remained strong. The timidity in Cameron now would not allow him to have conversations with his mother who remained blunt verbally. He tip-toed to have conversations with her and only asked for things if he really needed it. He walked on eggshells around her and other adults. The adults around him did not understand him because he used a smile and corny jokes as a way to mask the pain he was enduring.

Outside of his timidity, Cameron learned the slang language from "the streets" as a way to communicate. He began doing things that were not the core values his mother taught him, but his actions oddly filled the void Cameron needed to be filled so badly. Unbeknownst to Cameron, his decisions were adding to his pain and trauma.

Cameron, still attending the alternative school, realized he enjoyed the smaller settings and individualized attention. With the support from school, the light he once had from an early age began to shine again. He began passing all of his classes and even graduated a year early.

As Cameron prepared for graduation, he received news that his father was found deceased. Cameron's father, the one he had been longing for his whole life, was listed as "John Doe" because he had been found without identification and lived isolated from everyone he knew. Cameron felt confused and more outraged than ever before. He wondered how this could even be happening?

After years of not seeing their father, Cameron, age 17, and his older sister get to see him in a casket. To make matters worse, Cameron's mother decided she would not be in attendance at the funeral due to familial disagreements in regards to arrangements. Once again, Cameron was devastated. Crying was an understatement. The boy let out a screech, pulled himself together, and the children went to their father's funeral. For many years after the funeral, Cameron would go to father's grave, cry, and tell him how much he hated him. This incident caused him to hold in his feelings, attempt to avoid reality, get into unhealthy relationships, and give up easily every time situations became too difficult.

After graduation, Cameron worked in an industrial plant for a little while, and was eventually laid off for attendance. On the weekends, he would rather hang out, party, drink, and smoke rather than work. Finally, at the age of 19, he started a job as a correctional officer. He saw the inmates in their cells and noticed they were hurt, angry, misguided, and full of voids that contributed to their mindsets of committing crime just like him. The sad reality is that some of the inmates had more mental and emotional freedom than Cameron, even though he could go home every night while he locked and unlocked their cells each day. Cameron's life began to change during his time working as a correctional officer at the maximum-security male prison when an inmate arrested for murder began to minister to him about God and life. He took the lessons to heart. This is where his mindset began to change step by step through seeking God, reading books, online research, general exposure to life, and being more willing to learn from others.

As we close out this chapter, I don't want to leave without saying Cameron's entire childhood was not all bad experiences. He enjoyed playing with his cousins, spending time outside, having large dinners, and attending cookouts with his family. His family also took him to church which gave him his first experiences with faith. With all this said, the traumatic experiences Cameron faced caused him not to see the value in the positive aspects of life like he should. The negative experiences took on a louder voice which overshadowed the way Cameron responded throughout the early parts of his life.

## *Write Your Story*

Below, I have left a space for you to REWIND and write your own story. It's best to write in chronological order. If you need to take a break during your writing, that's perfectly fine! Just be sure to come back later to complete your writing after you have digressed.

_____
_____
_____
_____
_____
_____
_____
_____
_____
_____
_____
_____
_____

# 14 | RESET

# CHAPTER 2
# EVALUATE/ REEAVALUATE

**Evaluate:** To determine or fix the value of; to determine the significance, worth, or condition of usually by careful appraisal and study. To judge or calculate the quality, importance, amount or value of something.

***Example of evaluate:*** *Doctors evaluate a patient's condition.*

**Reevaluate:** Evaluate again or differently (Especially with regard to changes or new information)

***Example of reevaluate:*** *If a child catches her father leaving a dollar under her pillow, it will make her reevaluate her belief in the Tooth Fairy.*

In this chapter, we will evaluate and reevaluate the traumatic events in Cameron's life to see how these experiences manifested and impacted Cameron.

| EVALUATE | REEVALUATE |
|---|---|
| Cameron's father was not present. | Cameron became disappointed and did not trust adults. |
| Cameron's father gave him false promises. | Cameron became angry because of the false promises. Cameron began disrespecting adults. |
| Cameron was sexually abused. | Cameron had great distrust for authority. He began wearing big clothing, acting like a gangster, and became promiscuous. |

| | |
|---|---|
| Cameron's mother appeared aggressive and was very strong in character. | Cameron learned to be quiet and hold his feelings in. When angry, he would explode. Cameron learned to be strong and never ask for help. |
| Cameron could not communicate with his mother. | He learned to not communicate in other relationships and felt that he did not have a voice. Cameron allowed others to take advantage of him. He learned to run from challenges when it was time to communicate and gave up easily when things became hard. |

| | |
|---|---|
| Cameron's mother worked long hours. | Cameron's sister took care of them. Cameron was free to roam the streets. Cameron learned to work hard. |
| Cameron began to fail school. | Cameron became depressed and repeated the 9th grade. He began hanging in "the streets" and talking slang. His education was not as important as the pain he felt. Cameron became angrier. |

| | |
|---|---|
| Cameron began hanging with the wrong crowd. | Cameron began getting in trouble in "the streets" with fighting, drugs, and sex. Although Cameron created more pain for himself and others, "the streets" showed Cameron love and attention. |
| Cameron saw his mother struggling financially. | Cameron felt less than because of it and would not ask his mother for the things he needed. Cameron felt bad for his mother but began treating girls poorly. |
| Cameron's father passed away. | This left Cameron angry and confused. |

| | |
|---|---|
| Cameron went to the alternative school. | Cameron did well academically with a smaller class size and more attention. Cameron also met other kids that were not making good decisions and began to hang with them. Cameron graduated school a year early. |
| Cameron had a large extended family and lots of cousins. The family always had gatherings with fellowship and food. | Cameron had hope and found laughter around them. |
| Cameron's mother took them to church. | Cameron found a sense of community and found people he could talk to. |

## *Now Let's Evaluate And Reevaluate Your Story*

| EVALUATE | REEVALUATE |
|---|---|
|  |  |
|  |  |
|  |  |
|  |  |

# CHAPTER 3
# RELEASE

In this chapter, we are going to discuss releasing the negative causes and effects from the EVALUATE AND REEVALUATE chapter. Although we are working to release our negative experiences, it is important to be intentional about highlighting the good in our lives, no matter how big or small it may seem, in order to help us further heal. The first thing we have to do is forgive. According to Webster's dictionary, the definition of forgiveness is to cease to feel resentment against (an offender); forgive one's enemies. I know you are probably saying forgive! No way! But hear me out. Think of a large rope holding you to a person or traumatic experience you have gone through. The more you try to move forward and accomplish your dreams, the harder you have to fight because you have that person's weight attached to you. The weight will cause more strain and pain on you emotionally. These are the same unhealthy emotions that we are wanting to release so that you can move forward. In other words, you forgive for yourself. That does not excuse what you have gone through or make an excuse for anyone that may have intentionally or unintentionally disappointed you. Forgiveness does not mean you have to continue to be around the person who hurt you if it endangers your life. In this case, seek help. With those you still have to be around, you will have to set boundaries or standards of respect to protect yourself.

DO THIS EXERCISE WITH ME:

1. Close your eyes.
2. Now think of the person, people or event(s) that disappointed you.
3. See yourself tied to the person, people or event(s) with a large rope.
4. Visualize yourself trying to walk forward while pulling them with you. By now, I imagine you feel the anger, tiredness, and weight of pulling them along.

5. Pause and take a deep breath.

6. Keep your eyes closed and visualize looking at the person, people or event(s) and say to them, *"I forgive you, let you go and I release you of all of the expectations I have or had of you in my life. You are imperfect and so am I. I release you so that I can be free to move forward."*

7. Visualize taking the largest scissors you can and cutting yourself free from that person without harming them or yourself. Now turn around and move forward.

One thing I want you to take note of is that after you cut the rope, forgave, and decided to move forward, pieces of the rope are still tied around your waist. The pieces left symbolize that you still have work to do to heal and untie yourself completely as you move forward. Don't be too hard on yourself. From time to time, the person, people, or event(s) may come to your mind. The good thing is that you are on your path to healing even if you make a few more mistakes based on your old way of thinking. Just repeat the above exercise, replace your thoughts and behavior with something positive, and move forward.

In this section I want you to write a letter to your younger self as the person you are today. Apologize for all that you have gone through, the mistakes you have made, and the anger you may have displayed and for the unhealthy decisions.

**Example**

Dear Cameron,

I apologize for all that you have gone through. If I were there, I would have protected you. I apologize for others disappointing and hurting you, for the nights you cried and went without, and for no one seeming to come to your rescue. I apologize on behalf of your father and mother. I apologize that no one believed you when you said you were being abused. I apologize for allowing my mind to be clouded, giving up on school, and treating others poorly. I give you permission to be free of all the hurt I have caused because I was hurt and confused. All the hurt was not your fault even though it is now your responsibility to heal. I hope others I have hurt can forgive me as well. As I write to you, I forgive myself as well. You are strong, beautiful, intelligent, and a leader with so much value. It's okay to love yourself and know that you are loved regardless of what you have gone through. You are free to move forward and create the life you want.

After writing the letter to your younger self, you may feel the need to write a short paragraph to someone else (a parent, guardian, friend, etc...) asking them to forgive you. Space has been provided below to write the letter and other paragraphs.

# 30 | RESET

Dear _____(Self)

_____

_____

_____

_____

_____

_____

_____

_____

_____

_____

_____

_____

_____

_____

_____

_____

_____

_____

_____

Dear _____

Dear _____

Dear _____

Dear _____

# CHAPTER 4
# RECOVER

**REWRITE YOUR STORY**

You may be asking what is there to recover. There is a lot to recover. This will be your last writing assignment.

Write a three-paragraph essay of what you want your life to look like.

Include your childhood, your family, how you want to treat others, how you want to be treated, your goals (short-term and long-term), your looks, and how you want others to see you.

As you write, visualize what it would look like. Keep in mind, life is not perfect and every human being will go through some things here on earth. As you continue to grow and mature, mistakes will be made. When you do, forgive yourself and others and correct your mistakes and decisions. Above all NEVER GIVE UP! No matter how tough life gets and no matter what life throws at you, NEVER GIVE UP!. You have the power, through your decisions, to create the life you want to give yourself the power you deserve.

**EXAMPLE**

My name is Cameron. I am 17 years old. I do not have a perfect life. It's just my mother, my sister, and myself. I do all I can to help my mother and sister because I see how hard my mother works to provide. I focus on my education and choosing good friendships because I want to stay safe and make her proud of all of her hard work. I will love and respect others because I know what it is to not have those things. Even though I do not have all that I want right now, I choose to be positive and focus on bringing my grades up and playing sports to keep me busy.

When I am angry or feeling down, I will listen to some music, go for a walk or run, or talk to someone I trust so I do not take my feelings out on others. One of my short-term goals is to get a job for the summer to help my mother and to purchase my own school clothes. I am determined to make the honor roll the entire upcoming school year to help me with receiving scholarships for college. One of my long-term goals would be to graduate college with my degree in Cyber Security.

I would like to purchase a home and have a family of my own. We would have stability and great communication. We would take trips during Summer and Spring break so I can show my kids things I did not get to see as a child.

# REWRITE YOUR STORY

_____
_____
_____
_____
_____
_____
_____
_____
_____
_____
_____
_____
_____
_____
_____
_____
_____
_____

# CHAPTER 5
# RESET

Congratulations!!!!! If you have taken the five lessons seriously (**REWIND**, **REEVALUATE**, **RELEASE**, **RECOVER** AND **REWRITE** YOUR STORY, **RESET**), you are on the way to healing and making great decisions for your life and others. This is your opportunity to experience the beginning of a better life and making better decisions, one decision at a time. I have included a list of affirmations below to continue to speak over and believe for in yourself as you move forward.

**DAILY AFFIRMATIONS**

- ✓ **I am strong.**
- ✓ **I succeed at everything I do.**
- ✓ **I am a leader.**

- ✓ **Nothing can stop me.**
- ✓ **I am not a victim.**
- ✓ **I am victorious.**
- ✓ **I love myself.**
- ✓ **I love others.**
- ✓ **I respect myself.**
- ✓ **I respect others.**
- ✓ **I will complete all of my goals.**
- ✓ **I communicate all my needs and desires.**
- ✓ **I know what to do.**
- ✓ **Others look up to me.**
- ✓ **I am beautiful inside and out.**
- ✓ **I take care of my everyday task.**
- ✓ **I set goals daily.**
- ✓ **I will not let myself down.**

- ✓ I am powerful.
- ✓ I can accomplish anything I put my mind to.
- ✓ Education in every form is important.
- ✓ I will be wealthy financially one day.
- ✓ I help those in need.
- ✓ Others can depend on me.
- ✓ I have others I can depend on.
- ✓ I speak positive words.
- ✓ I influence others with my words.
- ✓ Today will be a great day.
- ✓ I put my best foot forward.
- ✓ I do my best.
- ✓ I forgive those who disappoint me.
- ✓ I forgive myself.
- ✓ I am kind to others and myself.

- ✓ I love life.
- ✓ Life has a lot to offer me.
- ✓ I have lots of gifts and talents.
- ✓ I am an awesome person.
- ✓ Those around me can see my light.
- ✓ I am an asset to those around me.
- ✓ I bring joy to others.
- ✓ I will not fear.
- ✓ I will not give in to peer pressure.
- ✓ I will not give up.

# ABOUT THE AUTHOR

## CYNNAMON CLINTON

**Cynnamon Clinton** is a woman that loves hard, because God has loved her unconditionally. She has over 23 years of law enforcement experience. She is currently a Special Victims Unit Investigator assigned as the liaison for SC Department of Social Services, foster care and emergency protective custody (abuse and neglect cases) coordinator for the Richland County Sheriff's Department. She is the **CEO** of **Generational Overcomers LLC**, where she helps individuals develop and strengthen social and emotional learning. She also focuses on those who have experienced childhood and relational trauma transition from trauma to transformation. She has written two books entitled "Generational Overcomer: No More Silence" and the workbook. She offers 6 and 12 lesson individualized or group coaching programs. She is a certified life coach and Transformational Mindset Speaker. She uses her experience of overcoming traumatic experiences and being labeled as an at-risk youth along with techniques as to how she overcame, to educate others. Cynnamon loves community outreach, helping others overcome difficult past experiences, traumatic experiences from life and relationships and working with youth. Cynnamon has received many awards and recognitions for her work in the community and with youth. She has an 18-year-old daughter, who is her best friend, and whom she cherishes very much.

www.generationalovercomers.com
Facebook: Generational Overcomers
Instagram: Generational Overcomer
Youtube: Generational Overcomers

**For More Information About Cynnamon Clinton and Generational Overcomers LLC:**

Visit Our Website: www.generationalovercomers.com

Like and Follow Us On Facebook: Generational Overcomers

Follow Us On Instagram: Generational Overcomer

Subscribe To Our Youtube Channel: Generational Overcomers

www.ingramcontent.com/pod-product-compliance
Lightning Source LLC
LaVergne TN
LVHW061042070526
838201LV00073B/5145